The Great Tapestry of Scotland

THE GREAT TAPESTRY OF SCOTLAND

The Great Tapestry of Scotland
The Making of a Masterpiece

Susan Mansfield and Alistair Moffat

BIRLINN

First published in Great Britain in 2013 by
Birlinn Ltd
West Newington House
10 Newington Road
Edinburgh
EH9 1QS

www.birlinn.co.uk

3

ISBN: 978 1 78027 133 0

British Library Cataloguing-in-Publication Data
A catalogue record for this book is available from the British Library

Designed by Mark Blackadder

Printed and bound in Britain by Bell & Bain Ltd, Glasgow

Contents

Preface

This is the story of a country and of how that story came to be told in an extraordinary and beautiful work of art. The details of how the Great Tapestry of Scotland came into existence are set out in this book by Alistair Moffat and Susan Mansfield. Their accounts describe how this is the result of the hard work and dedication of many hundreds of people throughout Scotland, the stitchers, but we must not forget that behind this great communal work there stand three people who should be regarded as the creators of this wonderful treasure: the artist, the narrator, and the maker. The artist is Andrew Crummy. In his quiet and modest way, Andrew is an artist who has brought great joy to many and in doing so has enriched the public life of Scotland. There is a loveliness and a resolution in his work that has an immediate beguiling effect on those who see it. His is a great hand, and Scotland is fortunate to see the results of its labours. This tapestry is, quite simply, a masterpiece, and it is Andrew's vision that lights it from the very first panel to the last.

Then there is the historical vision. This tapestry has a narrative, and that is the creation of a writer, Alistair Moffat, who has a profound understanding of Scottish history and who has the ability to communicate that understanding to people. Alistair has told Scotland's history here with fairness, honesty and good humour. People love to discuss the interpretation of the past, and the history of the Scottish nation, which sometimes delights in argument, is a well-known minefield. But what Alistair has achieved here is a dignified and balanced account of an often troubled history. Most importantly, it is a story that is told with love – and that shows.

The maker is Dorie Wilkie. The telling of Scotland's story here is a matter of needle, thread and linen. Andrew's drawings and Alistair's narration had to be translated into physical expression, and it is this process that Dorie, as co-ordinator and supervisor of the stitching, has handled so expertly. She has guided the hundreds of hands that have made this tapestry. She has encouraged and cajoled, inspired and taught the volunteers who have given so much of their time to create this magnificent object. Her influence shines through the whole work.

There are many others who have done so much to create this result, that it would be impossible to thank them all. But here it is: we have it now – an inspiring and beautiful thing, an expression of love for a country, a gift from many hundreds of people to those who will see it and enjoy it in the future. Please look at it, whether you see it in the flesh or in the photographs in this book. Please enjoy it and think of the lives of the people whose story it tells. This tapestry brings us face to face with them and reminds us, I think, of who we are and of what our history means. The people we see in this tapestry are, after all, ourselves.

ALEXANDER McCALL SMITH

Introduction

For two years a thousand needles have pricked panels of pristine linen and pulled a thread through our history. Working in small groups all across the nation, from Shetland to Galloway and from Argyll to the Buchan, volunteers sat down to stitch together a story of Scotland; to make a tapestry for a nation, something never before attempted. Its brilliance is startling. Rich but subtle colour makes the designs come instantly alive. A world of intricacy lies unseen behind it. A repertoire of stitches such as Lazy Daisy, French Knots, the Cretan Stitch, Heavy Chain and a score of others, the clever hands of the makers, the sweep, the brio of the drawing and its sureness of touch all combine to tell an old story and make it seem new and fresh.

But it is not really new, and although the achievement is glorious, it is not really a tapestry. But neither is Bayeux. More precisely they are both huge pieces of narrative embroidery that share many of the characteristics, impact and convenience of tapestries. Dating from the third century BC – and probably some time before then – these stories of thread and fabric have been made for millennia. Used as decoration, bursts of colour in an otherwise dreich hall, chamber or church, they also had a useful role as draught excluders in an age before well-fitting windows, doors or insulation. And they were portable. Once a court or a noble family moved on (these items were an expensive luxury), their servants would simply roll up a tapestry and re-hang it in whichever castle or palace they arrived at next.

The Bayeux Tapestry had another function beyond keeping out the draughts. Made in France at the behest of Odo, Bishop of Bayeux, it records the victory of his half-brother, William the Bastard, Duke of Normandy, at Hastings in 1066. Deeply political, it sought to tell a certain version of history and it could be hung as a vivid reminder of the dominance of the Norman elite. Its power is enduring – but not only because it is a fascinating series of freeze-frames, a unique record of a pivotal moment in European history. It exerts a greater, more mysterious pull, something shared by all great tapestries. Somehow these sumptuously fabricated pieces of cloth reach out across centuries and, inviting close examination, they draw in those who gaze at the figures, the landscape and the gorgeous decoration. Tactile (but please don't), tapestries tap into history perhaps because they have been made by human hands and brains, and they depict events brought back to life not on the page or the screen but in an object of great intrinsic beauty.

The Great Tapestry of Scotland was Sandy McCall Smith's idea. Gifted, generous and great-hearted, he was inspired by the lovely Prestonpans Tapestry, the artistic child of Andrew Crummy. Once Sandy had recruited him, he called me. My office phone is ancient, bright red, very loud with an alarm-clock ring, and also ex-directory. When Sandy rang, the day after he saw the Prestonpans Tapestry, I jumped out of my seat, having been scribbling something, mustering what passes these days for concentration. Now I can't remember what I was doing, because within ten seconds I accepted Sandy's flattering invitation to choose what might make up the panels of a tapestry that told Scotland's story. And we all took the first steps on a long, wonderful, emotional and unexpected journey.

Andrew Crummy is a great artist, simple as that, and this huge project is – up to now – his crowning achievement. I loved working with him, visiting his pleasingly cluttered, creative, crazy studio in Cockenzie, talking endlessly about what we could and couldn't do, about what stitchers liked to stitch, about language and about beginnings and endings. I met Dorie Wilkie, the Head Stitcher, who has overseen such a display of conspicuous quality, her own skills guiding others with a discerning but kind eye. And Gillian Hart has beautifully organised and marshalled what could so easily have been a ramshackle of bits and pieces, promises and uncertainties. None of this would have come to pass without Jan Rutherford and Anna Renz. Not only have they done a mountain of work on the press and public relations for the project, they also raised the bulk of the cash to pay for this flood of creativity. It has been a pleasure beyond measure to work with such a talented group.

To make a tapestry for a nation, something without helpful precedent, involves a glorious process of ruthless editing. Pitfalls yawn open on every side. One of the deepest is the military option, the temptation to see our history as a series of invasions, wars and battles, many of them grey defeats. And then to sprinkle a few saints, poets and inventions into the gaps, the times when swords and spears were silent. Another is to show Scotland and the generations of nameless people who made the landscape and built the towns and cities as a soft-focus background chorus for colourful, stately aristocratic processions. While some pivotal set-pieces simply insist on inclusion, such as Bannockburn and the Jacobite Risings, other episodes in our history that have rarely ventured onstage now rightly claim a place: the great timber halls of prehistoric farmers at Balbridie on Deeside, at Claish in Perthshire and at Kelso; James Small and his world-changing invention of the swing-plough and the story behind Donald MacIver's heart-breaking lyric, *An Ataireachd Ard*. Most important have been our collective efforts to make a tapestry that distils Scotland's unique sense of herself, to tell a story only of this nation, the farthest north-west edge of Europe, a place on the edge of beyond. And, without bombast, pomp or ceremony, to ask the heart-swelling rhetorical question: Wha's Like Us?

And it is Us, We, the Scots, Wirsells, Oorsells, Sinn Fhein, all of the Inhabitants, who are the proper subject of this great tapestry of Scotland. More than ten years ago, I wrote a long history of my own native place, the Scottish Borders, and I gave the last chapter the baffling title of Oo. It is Border Scots for We or Us. When I came back home, having spent twenty wasted years in the wilderness, in Edinburgh, I noticed that Borderers often used the word Oo. 'Oo never worried aboot the weather on common ridin' mornin'. Oo're gan, rain or no.' Or 'They Edinburry folk aye think oo're aa donnert, slow, like.'

It seemed to me, then and now, that this story of Oo signifies a strong sense of community as well as a lack of individual confidence. It may also be a symptom of a slowly dying habit from the past. Whatever the origin, Scotland still appears to me to retain a powerful, complex, collective sense of itself. Its people still see themselves as various sorts of Oo, and while we might bicker entertainingly amongst ourselves, Glasgow and Edinburgh, Highland and Lowland, if ever an outsider, particularly one from the south, offers a critical word, Oo will turn as one on them.

This interlocking, contradictory, fissiparous and mysterious aspect of Scottishness was something Andrew Crummy and I thought about a great deal as we worked in the early days of this project. Without ever being blunderingly explicit, we

both understood that the panels had to tell a story of all of
the people, the people who came north after the long millennia of the ice, the people who first saw the great rivers, the
mountains, the firths and the sea lochs; the people who made
Scotland over eleven thousand years. That is why the panels
are almost all dominated by figures, images of men and
women that are often hieratic, with bold profiles, or images
of groups interwoven or attached. Human movement animates
the narrative everywhere, making it march on down the
centuries to reach us here and now at the outset of the twelfth
millennium of our continuous history. It could equally have
been called the Great Tapestry of the Scots. After all it has
been made by a thousand Scots and its scale is epic, nation-
wide. As Andrew Crummy's drawings went out to addresses
in Shetland, Lewis, Aberdeenshire and all postcodes south to
Galloway and the banks of the Tweed (and to some exiles,
poor souls), we realised that this was the biggest community
arts project ever undertaken in Scotland.

As Andrew and I talked about the drama of battle, change,
loss and invention, and how these flashpoints could be fitted
into the more important everyday dramas of the lives of
ordinary people, we began to think about how the panels
could comprehend those. How could we show something of
the day-in, day-out labour of women and men raising and
providing for children, of men and women wringing a living
from the hungry soil, risking their lives on the fishing boats
and down the mines and in the patchwork of work all over
the story of our nation? But rather than create an artificial
historical frame, we decided simply to show it. Between panels
depicting incidents, saints, the famous and the notorious, there
appear generic panels with images of people working, walking
their lives under Scotland's huge skies. And they are simple
and eloquent, needing little explanation.

Early Scotland is also – conventionally – a story of men.

My own work in DNA studies and elsewhere has led me to believe that in the millennia before the last two centuries, the status of women was little better than that of informal slavery. And so Andrew and I took every opportunity to include female figures wherever figures were needed, both in the specific and generic panels. Clann-Nighean an Sgadain is a good example. They were the Hebridean Herring Girls who followed the fishing fleets in the 19th and early 20th centuries to gut and barrel the herring catch as it came ashore around Scotland's ports. We did not distort our national story to include women where they were not actors in events, but we recognised that always they were there, giving life to the nation, and we tried never to forget that.

Not that we would have been allowed to. Almost all of the stitchers are women and they would not have let us do anything less. That fact remains an absolutely determinant influence. Andrew and I talked of renaissance altarpieces and the predella panels that were often attached below the main image of the Virgin and Child, or a crucifixion or the Adoration of the Magi or whatever the donor had chosen. We decided that panels could and should have similar spaces so that the groups of stitchers could add images important to them and their part of Scotland. That has worked wonderfully well – and they are all images chosen and created by Scotland's women. The stitchers have also occasionally challenged me and my choices and one impatient email about those in 'the foothills of Pedantia' was inadvertently sent to the wrong address. Well, it wouldn't be Scotland without the occasional rammy.

This beautiful place has also shaped the tapestry. Geology made the landscape and the landscape formed the character of the people. Andrew Crummy and the stitchers have understood this perfectly and his and their images have been given life and substance with all the subtle colours of the land, the browns, greys, blues and the deep pigments of plants and the ever-changing weather. They need no maps to speak of all Scotland. Just as Harris Tweed is unmistakably of Harris and the Hebrides, and Border Tweed is from the rolling hills of the south and their moods and colours, what the stitchers have achieved in sewing together a physical sense of our nation is wholly remarkable.

Uniquely, Scotland comes alive in this tapestry in ways that are glorious but essentially mysterious.

ALISTAIR MOFFAT

AN GORTA MOR

FIRST OLD FIRM GAME

IRISH IMMIGRATION AFTER THE FAMINE
FOUNDING OF CELTIC AND RANGERS FOOTBALL CLUBS

TRINITY
STITCHERS

The Making of a Masterpiece

All over Scotland, handovers have been taking place. Packages have changed hands in doorways, on kitchen tables, in coffee shops, at the school gates, rolled up, wrapped in cloth, folded inside Marks & Spencer carrier bags. One even made its way back and forth on the ferry between Harris and North Uist, watched over by the crew. Precious packages. Packages of craftsmanship, packages of history.

Stitchers from all over the country have worked on the Great Tapestry of Scotland. More than 420 million years of history have been broken down into panels one metre square, and placed with groups of volunteers, from Shetland to the Borders, passed from hand to hand as each member takes their turn. Each panel tells a fragment of a larger story, from the first settlers to the reconvening of the Scottish Parliament, from Bonnie Prince Charlie to Archie Gemmill, from Mary, Queen of Scots to the Higgs boson. Here is the story of Scotland: kings and commoners, rebellions and inventions, heroes and disasters. Remove any of the 165 panels and the story is incomplete. And behind it there is another story, woven between the lines, the story of more than 1,000 people who have stitched; the story of one of the most ambitious community art projects ever undertaken in Scotland.

This story – our story – begins with a man looking at a tapestry. He is the writer Alexander McCall Smith and, on a chilly November day in 2010, he is visiting an exhibition of the Prestonpans Tapestry at Edinburgh's Dovecot Studios. The recently completed tapestry is itself a triumph: 104 metres of embroidered linen created by more than 200 volunteer stitchers, telling the story of Bonnie Prince Charlie's campaign which brought him to a historic victory over Government troops at Prestonpans in 1745. Sandy was captivated by the detail and the craftsmanship, but he was also watching the audience. He remembers: 'At the same time as looking at the tapestry, I was also looking at the faces of the people looking at it, seeing everybody's sheer delight in this wonderful object.'

In a world where technology brings communication to our fingertips, we don't expect to be bowled over by the power of stitching. The narrative tapestry – of which the Bayeux Tapestry is the most famous example – is an old craft with a long history, but it has power, even today (technically crewel work, not tapestry, but the term has stuck). Sandy says: 'I think it goes way, way back to our first experience of art, cave painting, which is telling a story in the same way; you can follow the sequence of events, there is something there which is very, very fundamental in the human appreciation of art. It speaks in a very direct and basic way to people. It's a classic example of pictures telling a story.'

Sandy has a talent for ideas, and not just in his novels. It was his idea, for example, in 1995, to start an orchestra for amateur musicians in Edinburgh. Now the Really Terrible Orchestra has triumphed at Cadogan Hall in London and the Town Hall in New York. Scale doesn't intimidate him; he dreams big. And so, he started to wonder, might a tapestry be created which tells the story of Scotland? Might it be stitched by the people of Scotland, and given to the nation?

Sandy is also a man who doesn't let a good idea go cold

Andrew Crummy, designer of the
Great Tapestry of Scotland.

before he acts on it. Within a week of seeing the Prestonpans
Tapestry he had enlisted Andrew Crummy, the Cockenzie-
based artist who designed it, and author and historian Alistair
Moffat to draft the story. With both on board, he established
the Great Scottish Tapestry Charitable Trust, with broadcaster
Jim Naughtie and publisher Hugh Andrew among its trustees.
The project was on its way.

But, in fact, our story begins earlier than that, with another
man looking at another tapestry. This time, the man is Gordon
Prestoungrange, the Baron of Prestoungrange, visiting the
Bayeux Tapestry in Normandy – another man unexpectedly
struck by the power of stitching, another man with a talent
for big ideas. Having encouraged the role of community art
projects in the regeneration of Prestonpans in the last two
decades, and having a particular interest in marking Bonnie
Prince Charlie's famous achievement, he had an idea for a
tapestry of his own. On his return, he put the idea to Andrew
Crummy, the artist behind the town's mural trail, to make a
tapestry which does for Prestonpans what Bayeux did for the

Battle of Hastings, but with one condition: it must be at least 79 metres long, nearly a metre longer than Bayeux.

In its early days, the Prestonpans Tapestry seemed to benefit from the fact that most people didn't quite believe it could happen. Had any of the organisers stopped to think about the enormity of what they were proposing, they might have taken fright. As it was, everyone proceeded with Gordon Prestoungrange's plan. Andrew sketched a sample, which was stitched by his wife, Carmel Daly ('We'd been married for twelve years and I didn't know she could stitch!') and a call was put out for stitchers through the press and local arts festival. 'I thought it was a mad idea, that nobody would want to do it,' admits the project's administrator, Gillian Hart. 'And in a fortnight we had about two hundred people.'

With no organisational precedent, the team had to develop a way of working from first principles. Stitchers were recruited from along the route of the Prince's campaign, and materials were sourced. One of the volunteers was Dorie Wilkie, a recently retired librarian with City & Guilds qualifications in Embroidery and Design and an interest in textile art. 'I read the advert for stitchers and I was a bit sniffy,' she admits. 'I said: "Don't they know it's an embroidery not a tapestry? Maybe I should get in contact." Gordon invited me to the first meeting, and I kept asking questions: how are you going to do this, have you a system in place to do that? Eventually he said, would you like to be in charge of the stitching, and I was so naive I just said yes.'

Less than two years after Gordon Prestoungrange's visit to Bayeux, and thanks to a herculean effort on the part of Dorie, Andrew, Gillian and the stitchers, the Prestonpans Tapestry was unveiled. It has since toured widely in Scotland and England and has been seen by more than 180,000 people. The town is now fund-raising to build it a permanent home in a Living History Centre in Prestonpans.

Stitching co-ordinator Dorie Wilkie.

But perhaps our story really begins much further back, almost 900 years ago, when Bishop Odo of Bayeux, the half-brother of William the Conqueror, commissioned a tapestry for his new cathedral to commemorate his relative's victory in the Battle of Hastings. The Bayeux Tapestry is still admired today for its scale and consistency, the quality of its workmanship and its value as a piece of history (albeit a rather partisan one).

It continues to inspire modern epic tapestries: the Overlord Tapestry, commissioned in 1968 to tell the story of the D-Day invasion of France, and now hanging in Portsmouth; the Hastings Embroidery, an ambitious multi-panel

The Bayeux Tapestry, the world's first 'historical' tapestry (Time & Life Pictures/Getty Images).

appliqué made in the 1960s, showing 900 years of British history since the Battle of Hastings, and the New World Tapestry, hanging in Bristol, telling the story of English colonisation attempts in the Americas.

In recent years, large-scale embroidery has made a resurgence as a way of commemorating specific histories and landmark events. The Quaker Tapestry, telling the story of Quakerism from the 17th century to the present, was worked on by four thousand men, women and children from 15 countries in the 1980s. The Fishguard Tapestry tells the story of the last invasion of mainland Britain in Pembrokeshire in 1797. Millennium tapestries were created in Leeds, the Isle of Harris and the Nottinghamshire village of Gotham. But so far none has attempted to tell the story of an entire nation, stitched by its people. Not until now.

The team on the Great Tapestry of Scotland were under no illusions about the scale of the undertaking. Designer

Andrew Crummy, stitch co-ordinator Dorie Wilkie and administrator Gillian Hart had all worked on the Prestonpans Tapestry, and aimed to put into practice the lessons they learned there. But, at the same time, they knew that the stakes were much higher. Not only was the project bigger in every sense, it was attempting a much more ambitious sweep of history. Dorie Wilkie was determined that, community project or not, the quality of the stitching would be higher than ever. 'I wanted the stitching level to evolve. If it's being given to the nation, you want people to look at it and say: "Wow, that's good." The skills are there, and they're being used, and now people can see that.'

The first challenge belonged to Alistair Moffat: that of producing a text which could be the basis for a visual history of Scotland from the last ice age to the year 2000. It would cover key themes and great individuals, but it would also be a story of common life, work, recreation, achievement, sport, culture, politics and social history. In addition to the brief he would write, an event at the Festival of Politics in August 2012 invited speakers including historian Tom Devine and journalist Rosemary Goring to nominate their suggestions for a Parliament of the Ancestors. Members of the audience were also invited to contribute. The results of this now fill four half panels, listing individuals from Saint Cuthbert to Lord Reith, Alexander Fleming to Norman MacCaig.

As Alistair worked on chopping the history of Scotland into suitable fragments, his text passed to Andrew Crummy, who was embarking on the most ambitious undertaking of his career to date. It was up to him to translate Alistair's text into images for stitching, to tell the story of Scotland in pictures. 'I'd go to bed at night and think, "Oh my god what have I taken on, this could be the end of me," but actually when I thought about it, I thought, "No, not really, I think I know what I'm doing." I'm a mural artist; I'm used to painting

250–300 feet of murals. I also grew up with community arts projects.'

Andrew's mother, Helen Crummy, had been the organising secretary of the Craigmillar Festival Society, and he grew up surrounded by her work. 'In Craigmillar, having three or four hundred people involved in a community arts project was actually quite a common thing; that was the essence of what she was about, and that is important to this project. In essence, it is a community arts project. It's not my vehicle to tell the world how I think about the history of Scotland. It's about creating something where lots of people can say this is what they think is important.'

Andrew trained in illustration at Duncan of Jordanstone College of Art & Design in Dundee and Glasgow School of Art, and began his commission by drawing the panels in miniature, like a movie storyboard. 'It's not illustration; it's visual storytelling, there is a difference. I think you've got to create something which is like a movie or a good book. People have got to be able to read it, there's got to be a clarity to it. Sometimes you can be clever, but it's not about being clever, it's about being clear. And often less is more; it's about summarising things.'

He needed to give the project a visual unity while still allowing space for individual expression. The same simple grid structure underlies all the designs and a few elements are kept constant from panel to panel. The intensity of detail on some panels is balanced by more spacious designs on others. Many of the panels have areas around the edges where the stitchers can contribute their own ideas. Andrew drew inspiration from medieval illuminated manuscripts and Pictish stones, bringing in Charles Rennie Mackintosh and Art Nouveau touches for the late-19th and early-20th century panels, and a more contemporary abstract design for later ones – a nod, perhaps, to Damien Hirst's spot paintings.

Opposite.
The Festival of Politics, 2012. Alexander McCall Smith, Alistair Moffat, Tom Devine, Andrew Crummy, Rosemary Goring and audience discuss who should feature in the Tapestry's Parliament of the Ancestors.

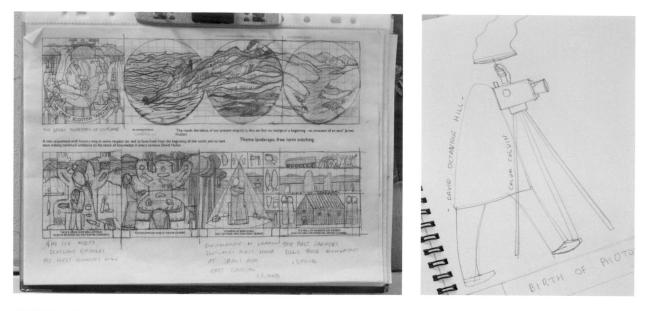

Andrew Crummy at work on the initial designs.

His biggest challenge was finding ways to condense major events and broad time periods into one metre of linen. 'The first two big panels are about the formation of the rocks of Scotland. How do you show thirty million years in two metres? Or "Scotland and its drive for empire", that's a huge subject. Some of the ideas are very difficult to visualise. How do you show the foundation of the Bank of Scotland, which is really about the creation of printed money? Or the formation of the NHS, or the resurgence of Gaelic?'

Then there are images so well known they are almost hackneyed (Bonnie Prince Charlie, Robert Burns), and the need to create variety within each period, so the Middle Ages are more than a sequence of battles, and the Victorian age not just a parade of middle-aged moustachioed gentlemen. And all the while, there is the pressure to get it right: is Dundee more famous for jam or marmalade? What is the difference between an Arbroath smokie and a Finnan haddie?

It required a particular attitude on the part of the artist because Crummy knew that he would be handing his designs over. By the time they had been reinterpreted by the stitchers they would no longer be his in the same way. 'The main thing is making it for stitch, so that the stitchers can show off and get involved. A lot of the ladies like to stitch clothes. You want to give them a vehicle so they can really show off, so you do Bonnie Prince Charlie's embroidered jacket, which is very traditional, but I was also doing things that were, to me, more interesting: oil rigs and Hillman imps, Archie Gemmill scoring his goal for the World Cup, bottles of Irn Bru, things you wouldn't normally see in stitching. It was important to have a sense of humour as well, because the Bayeux Tapestry has a lot of humour in it.'

To balance the humour, there would also be some sombre moments: a Black Death panel, with untended animals, ruined fields and a central figure curled in on herself with pain, acknowledgement of Scotland's less than savoury involvement in areas such as slavery. 'The history of Scotland isn't all positive; it's complex, we were involved in lots of things. We haven't gone for the heroic Scot, and it's not political, it's not part of the independence debate, we're not taking sides.'

As Andrew continued to fill books with drawings, the first call went out for stitchers at Borders Book Festival in June 2011. It was picked up by local press and broadcasters. Letters were sent to local embroiderers' guilds all over Scotland, and anyone connected with the project going on holiday in Scotland that summer took printed publicity with them. Within a comparatively short time, more than 500 people had responded, and in the months that followed the numbers continued to grow.

'We quickly realised we were going to have too many people to give them a panel each,' says Gillian Hart, who collated the names of all those who applied. 'Some people were in groups already, and we worked to put together other groups of people who lived in the same area. We tried,

An early gathering of stitchers at the Borders Book Festival.

wherever we could, to make sure that less experienced stitchers had a more experienced stitcher with them.'

Meanwhile, Dorie Wilkie was on a mission to find the best materials for the project. The linen on which the tapestry would be stitched was crucial, both for the stitchers and for the finishing and exhibiting of the panels. An online search led her to Peter Greig & Co in Kirkcaldy, Scotland's only surviving linen mill. The family-run company has been operating since 1825 in a town which, at its height, had 15 mills. It currently employs 32 people making a range of standard and bespoke fabrics, mainly for soft furnishings. Dorie visited and options were considered. Pure linen is the classic fabric for the job, but Dorie was concerned that it might crease too easily and require ironing every time the panels were moved, and a cotton-linen fusion was chosen, in an oatmeal colour, to complement the natural tones of the wools. Next up was thread. Dorie and the team considered wool spun in Scotland by small producers, but knew they needed a steady supply of consistent products and matching colours, and in the end the decision was taken to use a large yarn producer, Appletons.

Meanwhile, Jan Rutherford and Anna Renz, who had come on board initially as publicists, took on the fund-raising and co-ordinating of the project. They set a fund-raising target of £250,000 to take the tapestry from its inception to its first exhibition, covering the cost of materials, premises and other basics. 'Because none of us had ever been involved in a project like this before, we had no idea how much we would need,' Jan Rutherford says. 'We were working on a wing and a prayer.' Discussions with the Scottish Parliament led to an early decision to unveil the tapestry there in September 2013, but that brought its own challenges. Though barely a panel had been stitched, there was a deadline.

At least Dorie Wilkie now had a studio to use as a base.

By the entry-phone of an unassuming business centre in Eskbank, a small sign reads: 'Great Scottish Tapestry'. Upstairs, there are work tables, custom-built light boxes and yarns stacked in neat plastic boxes according to shade. There is also a notice which reads, optimistically, 'Now panic and freak out'. In the next few months, the space would become known to everyone involved in the project simply as 'The Hub'.

Jan Rutherford (left) and Anna Renz (right), Tapestry publicists and fund-raisers.

As Andrew's designs were completed and reviewed by Alistair, they were passed to Dorie and her team of volunteers who traced the designs onto linen and made up packs for stitchers with the panel, a coloured illustration and a selection of wools. Thinking ahead to the life and preservation of the tapestry, Dorie wrote advice for stitchers about keeping the fabric taut while stitching, always using frames. 'This is highly unusual, to work with an embellished surface, and to have different people work at different tensions. We have to think about everything: how is this going to hang? What's the best

The Hub, Eskbank, where the whole project was co-ordinated.

The last stitching pack is ready
to be posted.

way to present this? There was a lot of background work going
on.'

The first stitch in the Great Tapestry of Scotland was made
in September 2012 by Tricia Marwick, the presiding officer
at the Scottish Parliament. As the first kits were sent out to
individuals and groups of stitchers across the country, it was
up to Dorie to work out how much support the stitchers
would need. Unlike on the Prestonpans Tapestry, they had
asked for sewing experience, but levels of experience varied
a great deal. Those close enough to Edinburgh were invited
to the Hub for workshops, and many of the others were
visited by Dorie or Gillian.

Some of those taking part were highly experienced stitchers with City & Guilds qualifications. Others were experienced in sewing – cross stitchers and dressmakers and weavers – but were comparatively new to crewel work. Textile artists and professional makers joined in to try their hand. Some of the stitchers – male and female – had learned embroidery at school but had done little since. Skills were learned and relearned, one stitcher to another, as work began on the tapestry. One speaks of 'the amazing skill hidden away in Scottish living rooms'. Skills which were normally private were being taken out and given a place to shine.

The stitchers of the Great Tapestry of Scotland are a

The first stitch is made by the Rt Hon. Tricia Marwick, Presiding Officer of theScottish Parliament. Alexander McCall Smith looks on.

The Tapestry takes shape: stitchers at work, and showing off their finished panels.

diverse bunch. Dorie says they are: 'Varying intellects and a thousand million interests, all competing, or working together, a true cross-section of society.' Many are women, but there are also a number of men and at least two husband-and-wife stitching teams. A rowing club signed up for a panel, as did a community choir. Nine stitchers joined a group in the little Argyll village of Port Appin ('Where are they coming from?' Dorie asks. 'Out of the sea?') In Caithness, two women sharing a panel live so far apart they had to post it to one another. In the little Borders village of Smailholm, six stitchers lived within walking distance and were sometimes passing on their panel three times in a day.

Susie Finlayson had recently given up her job in IT with the University of Edinburgh when she volunteered to help trace panels and make up packs for stitchers at the Hub. But she had no intention of stitching herself. 'I had been helping

Susie Finlayson, key member of the Hub team.

Kate Edmunds, another
key Hub volunteer.

at the Hub for months, tracing and making up packs to send
to stitchers all over Scotland, and all the time I kept saying:
"Knitting and cross-stitch is my thing; I don't do embroidery
and crewel work." Then, just before Christmas, Dorie
presented me with a panel and told me to get on with it.
Fortunately, I had picked up a lot from her and the other
stitchers. I bought a book and gave it a go.'

   Kate Edmunds, another volunteer at the Hub, got drawn
into the Prestonpans Tapestry because she is Andrew
Crummy's neighbour. She is a keen felter and spinner, but had
never stitched before. 'I don't know how embroidery missed
me but it did; it just never crossed my path. I thought it was
all tablecloths and antimacassars. When the Prestonpans Tapestry was just beginning, Andrew's wife Carmel was doing a
test panel but she didn't have much time, so she taught me
three stitches and asked me to do as much as I could. I never
looked back. When she came back to get the panel, there was
no way I was going to give that panel up.'

Veronica Ross, the tireless organiser of the Smailholm stitchers, is retired from a career managing computer systems for the NHS, and admits she had little experience of crewel work. 'I know it sounds ridiculous, but I don't really do embroidery. I do sewing – we discovered that six of us in the Smailholm group had made our own wedding dresses. I liked the idea of being involved. They said basic stitching was required, so I took that at face value. Fortunately two of our group of twelve were really good embroiderers, and they guided us.'

Jim Mulrine had never considered himself to be stitcher. A time-served upholsterer who worked in the Clydebank shipyards on the interiors of ocean liners, he heard about the tapestry when following up his own interest in the medieval philosopher and theologian John Duns Scotus. 'As an upholsterer, I'm familiar enough with needles, but I didn't sign up because I wanted to make a tapestry; I did it because I was interested in one of the characters that one of the panels was going to be about.'

Unfortunately, the Duns Scotus panel, one of the first to be drawn full-size, had already been allocated, and when Jim found himself matched with a group of four lady stitchers working on a panel about the founding of the birth of the STUC, he faced a dilemma. 'I thought, what do I do? Do I back out now? I thought about it. But the tapestry was about Clydeside. I'd worked in the shipyards, I knew a bit about that, so I thought I'd carry on. Once I'd got a hold of it, had a go, I was actually quite comfortable. It was a good learning experience and they allowed me to work within my own limitations. We were able to do the best we could and be proud of the fact that we were able to do it.'

Jim says it proves that the notion of egalitarianism is at the heart of the Scottish psyche. 'People ask what makes Scottish people friendly, what makes them have a sense of

Early examples of stitching style.

who they are. It comes from our history, a sense that every-body is equal. That's why I'm able to go in and sit down with these four women and do a job. I see them as equal; I hope they see me as an equal to them. I don't see them as less than me or better than me, and that allows me to participate. That's part of our national personality.'

But it's one thing to sign up for the Great Tapestry of Scotland in a whirlwind of enthusiasm, and quite another to be confronted with a metre square of cream-coloured linen with the outline of a design on it. Group after group describe unwrapping their panel for the first time, staring at it and wondering where to start. The fact that you had been entrusted with a fragment of Scotland's history added to the nerves. Even expert stitchers were floored by it. 'I was shaking as I made the first stitch,' admits Mary Richardson, a veteran of the Prestonpans Tapestry and a stitcher with many years' experience.

With Kate Edmunds, Shona McManus and Elizabeth (Betty) Raymond, she formed a group called the Crewel Chicks'n'Dave. 'Dave is my husband,' laughs Mary. 'He did help out a lot – he didn't do any stitching but he did every-thing else.' The Crewel Chicks were allocated the panel celebrating geologist James Hutton and his theory of the Earth. Sometimes described as the father of modern geology, Hutton noticed the 'unconformity' of the rocks at Siccar Point in Berwickshire, and took that as conclusive proof of his theory of geological development.

'Most people know who James Hutton is but they don't know anything about him, even if they live in Berwickshire,' says Richardson. 'I didn't, and I was born in Eyemouth.' They turned to the Internet for information, and organised a field trip to Siccar Point, where Kate 'promptly freaked out because I don't really do heights' and they ended up toasting the project with (non-alcoholic) wine back at the car. However,

Opposite.
Members of the Clydeside Five show off their panel.

43

The Crewel Chicks 'n' Dave with their panel at Siccar Point.

Hutton's rocks provided plenty of opportunities for interesting stitching. Mary set herself a challenge to see if she could include a stitch in the panel with every letter of the alphabet, searching in books and on the internet to find the more unusual letters. 'We were so excited when I found Van Dyke stitch!' she says.

In Newport-on-Tay, a group who made crafts to sell for local charities were looking for a new project. Ursula Doherty's friends from Edinburgh came across the leaflet requesting

JAMES HUTTON'S THEORY OF THE EARTH.
SICCAR POINT, BERWICKSHIRE

From start to finish: the progress of the Sew for Dough Group's panel,
The Discovery Sails from Dundee (Dawn White Photography).

volunteer stitchers for the tapestry and, with their encouragement, she applied and was successful. Thanks to Dorie's policy of allocating place-specific panels to those who lived in the same geographical area, the group were allocated 'The Discovery Sails from Dundee'. They were delighted as this local landmark is just across the river from Newport and Wormit, where they all live.

On a field trip to *The Discovery*, they were particularly interested in the clothes worn by the crew: mid-brown canvas oilskins and sealskin gloves, and they were inspired to use Ghiordes Knots to create gloves with a furry texture. Andrew Crummy was happy to add two emperor penguins to the design as it had been this expedition which discovered the emperor colony at Cape Crozier. Also, motifs depicting The Nine Trades of Dundee were added along with the Newport-on-Tay Victorian drinking fountain, which became the group's emblem.

Then it was time to get stitching. Plans were made, weekly meetings minuted, numbered colour charts and a sewing rota drawn up and stitches practised. Dawn White, a photographer, documented the progress with weekly photographs on her blog. 'Once we had completed the outlining and filled in the four crew members we felt more confident,' says Dawn. 'Soon we were enjoying making headway despite our initial nervousness at being part of the Great Tapestry of Scotland. We felt privileged to be involved!'

Meanwhile, across the Tay in Dundee, Alister Rutherford was part of a team working on the 'Juteopolis' panel about the industries of Victorian Dundee. Alister took up stitching when he retired from a job in adult education with Angus Council in 2007 and quickly discovered a liking for bargello work, a style inspired by Florentine design involving blocks of flat stitches laid in a mathematical pattern. He applied to take part in the Great Tapestry of Scotland after his wife heard about it

Opposite.
Andrew Crummy's drawing for Panel 114.

JAM

JOURNALISM

JUTE

JUTEOPOLIS

THE SINKING OF HMY IOLAIRE OFF STORNOWAY 1919

on the radio. 'I was stitching away and she came running through to tell me that Alexander McCall Smith had said there weren't any men and that I should find out about it.'

He was invited to join up with three lady stitchers in Dundee, but says they were all rather daunted when the panel finally arrived. 'It was a bigger piece of work than any of us had ever done before and I'm not sure if any of us had stitched on linen – I hadn't and it was a daunting task. The fact that it was a big national project meant there was a little bit of stress. If you're just doing your own work and you make a mistake it doesn't matter, you can cut it up and throw it away, but working in a group, you don't want to let anybody else down.'

Once they got into their stride, however, they enjoyed it, and when it came to coming up with suggestions for additional images relating to Victorian Dundee, they weren't short of ideas. Those they proposed ranged from the Tay Bridge Disaster to Keiller's marmalade, and buildings such as the Royal Victoria Arch, demolished in the 1960s, and the McManus Galleries. 'We did it without thinking what it would be like to stitch,' says Alister. 'There is some quite intricate stuff, particularly with the buildings; we've made it harder for ourselves. We've also spent a lot of time researching, finding out what buildings looked like 150 years ago because we wanted it to look as accurate as possible – it all adds to the fun and excitement.'

Meanwhile, on the Isle of Harris, Gillian Scott-Forrest was unwrapping the panel about the sinking of the *Iolaire*. The Admiralty yacht, carrying back home to the Hebrides troops who had fought in the First World War, sank within sight of Stornoway harbour on 1 January 1919 with the loss of 205 lives. It remains one of the worst maritime disasters in UK waters in the 20th century.

When Gillian began to speak to islanders about the *Iolaire*, she was surprised how raw the emotion was, nearly 100 years on. 'Even to this day, some people choke up with tears and can't talk about it. I knew it would be painful, but I was astonished how real the emotion still is. I think we have to convey that to other people. All along there was a real rawness in what we were trying to depict; we had to not only communicate the history faithfully, we had to be sensitive to people who are still affected by it. Because it is a very sombre subject, the whole design has not leant itself to fancy, showy work. The stitches we've used are very simple, the drama comes from the colour and density we've put into the sewing.'

The group visited the *Iolaire* memorial, close to the rocks where the boat went down; Stornoway Town Hall, where the reports of the tragedy are kept, and Sandwick Cemetery where the dozen or so men are buried whose bodies were never identified. With Andrew Crummy's help, they sensitively portrayed scenes of the disaster around the main image, including the strong hands of John F. Macleod, who swam ashore with a rope and saved around 40 lives, and the ship's bell, which remains on the Isle of Lewis.

Gillian, who was the organiser of the Harris Millennium Tapestry, planned to work with fellow Harris stitcher Tracey MacLeod, but when they were joined by Moira MacPherson from South Uist, the logistics became more complicated. 'In January, bad weather disrupted ferry sailings and neither myself nor Moira could risk travelling in case we couldn't get a ferry home. So I wrapped the panel in a box and talked to the ferry crew, asked them to put it somewhere safe and hand it over to Moira, who would meet the ferry. They were very obliging, but it was worrying putting it on the ferry by itself; I could only relax when she phoned and said she'd got it.'

Over in Killearn, Lyn Dunachie and the members of the Strathendrick Embroidery Guild were wrestling with a double challenge, one of the few double panels in the tapestry, and one of Andrew's most abstract designs. The words of the Gaelic

song *An Ateareachd Ard* ('The Surge of the Sea') feature in Gaelic and English, along with an allegorical figure rising from the water symbolising the resurgence of Gaelic culture, her body shaped like a cello. The design has lots of the large flat areas embroiderers tend to dread. 'In the design she was coloured in yellow, but it was a big area, and I thought, "What am I going to do?"' says Lyn. 'I mentioned it to Dorie and she said, "Why don't you cover her with wild flowers?" And I thought that was a brilliant idea.' The figure is now covered with a soft pattern of the flowers used to produce natural yellow dye, with double-helix DNA strands in her long, red hair.

'Someone else commented that the sky was empty, there were no birds, could I not put in a skein of geese?' Lyn continues. 'So I asked Andrew and he sent me some geese. But then Dorie's husband Tom suggested I make one of them into a puffin – he wanted something jokey in it. I thought a puffin would be too small, so he said, how about a flamingo? In the end there are three flying mallards at the end of the skein of geese; they're not very noticeable, and a little bit of humour doesn't do any harm.'

Meanwhile, an even bigger challenge was being faced up the road in Dunblane where a group of four stitchers opened their panel and found themselves face to face with Archie Gemmill. 'I think our collective hearts sank into our boots,' says group leader Ann Gambles. 'None of us knew one end of a football from the other. It has been quite an education.'

They turned to Google for assistance and found pictures of the legendary goal scored in the World Cup match against the Netherlands in 1978, which – temporarily – gave Scotland a fighting chance at the title. They also discovered that a football is not just a football. 'Do you know there is a website where you can find the exact design of the ball from every World Cup every played?' says Ann, still incredulous. 'It

The Allanwater Stitchers
with Panel 150.

changes every time. The one we have embroidered is anatomically correct.' They also sourced an Umbro logo from 1978 for Gemmill's strip.

But stitching the man of the match proved to be just the beginning of their adventure as they went in search of images to put around the edges of the panel, relating not only to football but to popular culture in 1978. Andrew had already sketched a punk rocker 'with exceedingly pink hair, a safety pin in his ear, studs round his neck and the Red Road flats growing out of his head', to which was added Rod Stewart, Dennis the Menace ('We looked up how he was drawn in the 1970s') and an authentic lager can from the period, complete with its 'lager lovely' (thanks to another comprehensive website).

56

'We had enormous fun stitching it,' says Ann. 'My admiration for Scotland as a football team has not exactly rocketed. That whole campaign was a damp squib, they cranked it up as a real possibility that Scotland might win, and when we actually got there it didn't happen like that, and everybody came home quite early with their tails between their legs. But I do wonder how many husbands will get dragged along to see the tapestry. I have a sneaky suspicion they might end up in front of our panel.'

A surprise of a different kind was in store for the stitchers of Tillicoultry – though at least they didn't have to walk very far to get a stiff drink. The Needles & Gins group, organised by professional kilt-maker Lesley Thorton, met weekly in an upstairs room in their local pub, the Wool Pack. 'Though we decided not to do any sewing there in case we spilled drinks on the tapestry,' Thornton says. Their panel celebrates the production of the Hillman Imp in Linwood, and the steelworks at Ravenscraig which supplied the factory.

'I still remember people's faces when I first took it up to the group,' says Thornton. 'Everyone was daunted by the scale of it. Some people were daunted by the subject matter – embroidery and cars didn't go together in their minds – but I was excited that it was quite modern and had bright colours.'

As has often been the case on the project, people discovered connections with their subject. 'It seemed like no one had a connection to Ravenscraig or Hillman Imps, but when we got talking about it, it was amazing. People were saying they had one, it was their first car, and they had stories about it, usually about it breaking down – we did think we might add steam coming out the back of one of them, because the engine was at the back and it was always overheating.'

As the project took shape, their confidence grew, and eventually they did break their golden rule and do some sewing in the pub. Bringing their own inventiveness to bear,

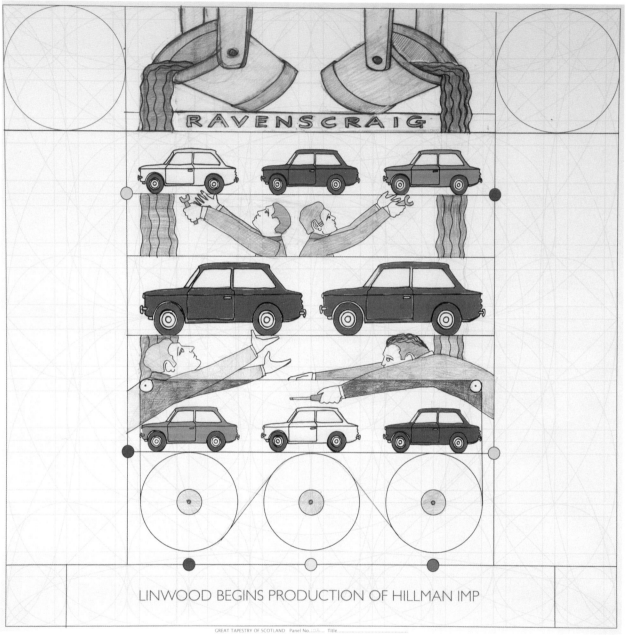

RAVENSCRAIG

LINWOOD BEGINS PRODUCTION OF HILLMAN IMP

GREAT TAPESTRY OF SCOTLAND Panel No........ Title..

Andrew Crummy's design for Panel 143.

The Tillicoultry Needles & Gins Group with their panel at the site
of the old factory at Linwood, birthplace of the Hillman Imp.

they individualised the cars on Andrew's production line, making one a police car Imp (previously in use in Dunbartonshire), another into a customised racing Imp, and a third – a nod to Lesley's profession – a tartan Imp. This is the only one of the cars shown in the panel which was never made, though a special edition Caledonian Imp did have some tartan in its upholstery.

Dorie Wilkie was well aware that the project was taking stitching into territory where it might never have been before, both in terms of stitching of large textured areas, like the sandstone frontage of St Andrews Cathedral, and in the specific objects which needed to be stitched. 'I mean, how do you stitch a rugby ball?' she laughs. 'I've never had to give it any thought before. How do you stitch a steel helmet? The ladies working on the Burke & Hare panel were saying, "I never thought I'd have to embroider a severed hand."'

Whatever their subject matter, the stitchers were meticulous about detail: the exact contours of the hills in the background at the Battle of Sheriffmuir, the colours in Suffragette tartan, the fabric of Ronnie Corbett's storytelling chair. In fact, there is more detail in the Great Tapestry of Scotland than any one visitor could take in: the lacework on a sleeve, the ermine on a royal robe, the darkening of a washerwoman's stained apron, the hawk soaring above Siccar Point, added because there is a hawk which hunts at the spot.

The Smailholm stitchers applied themselves, reluctantly at first, to the study of their subject, 'The Border Reivers and Kinmont Willie'. 'Our expert embroiderers are very good at pretty dresses and flowers and I think they had hoped to get something pretty,' says Veronica Ross. 'Most of us knew very little about the Border Reivers although we live in the shadow of a beautifully preserved reiver's tower. Once we got into the history, it's fabulous stuff, and we quickly became quite fond of our Reivers.'

The Smailholm Group and details of Panel 45.

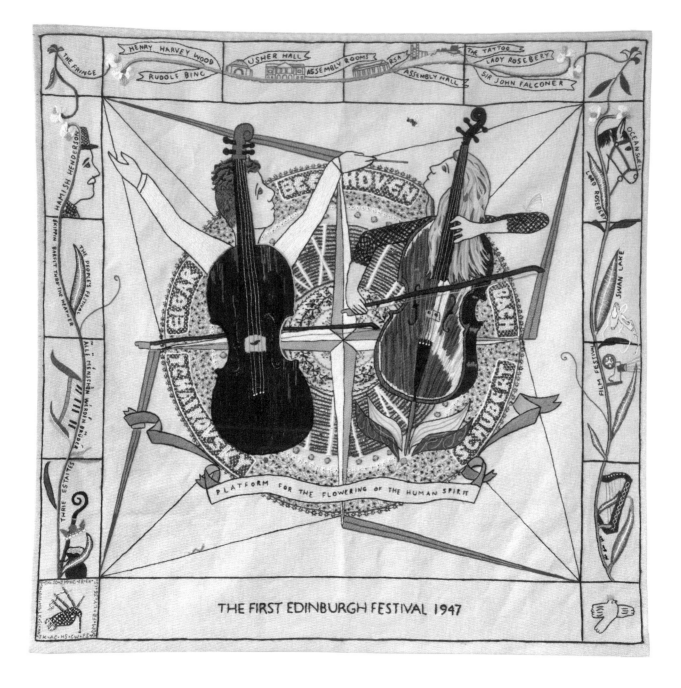

THE FIRST EDINBURGH FESTIVAL 1947

Reivers typically farmed in the summer and, on dark winter nights, went on lengthy expeditions to steal one another's sheep and cattle, occasionally progressing to arson and murder (the words 'bereaved' and 'blackmail' come from reiver times). They escaped the law by fleeing into the 'debatable lands' between Scotland and England, riding great distances on their sturdy Welsh ponies. Their reign of terror in the borderlands extended for over 300 years, and they are the subject of a splendid curse written by Gavin Dunbar, the Archbishop of Glasgow, which was read from every pulpit in Scotland in 1525.

Kinmont Willie was a notorious reiver who was captured in 1596 on an agreed Day of Truce, and made a daring and successful escape from Carlisle Castle. Willie was an Armstrong, the line from which astronaut Neil Armstrong is descended. As he died while the panel was being stitched, the group wanted to include a memento, and settled on adding the moon – 'but a winter moon, because that's when they went reiving'.

Veronica Ross is ultimately pleased that the Reivers will have their place in the stitched history of Scotland 'It's an amazing story, they were very resilient people; they had to survive in difficult times. It's important that their story is told. I wonder why we don't know more about them. It has changed the way I see the Borders landscape. I can begin to see how they got away with it for so long; it could only happen in a geography like this.'

It is remarkable how often, by accident or by design, the interests of the stitchers have married up with material in their panel. The panel commemorating the first Edinburgh Festival was stitched by a group based in and around Eskbank, many of whom are musicians. Stitchers included clarsach player Patsy Seddon, viola player and singer Mairi Campbell – perhaps best known for singing 'Auld Lang Syne' on the *Sex and the*

City movie with her band The Cast – and various talented amateur musicians. Mairi's sister, Ann, who organised the group, is a keen cellist. Patsy was able to stitch her own instrument into the design, the traditional Scottish clarsach, rather than the orchestral harp, which might be more typical for the Edinburgh Festival. Patsy says: 'It seems appropriate that one of the panels that's musically linked ended up with a big group of musicians. The Festival is known for its orchestral, classical, more high-brow music, but the panel does mention other things – the Fringe, folk music. Some of the musicians in the group have done orchestral playing, and some are involved in traditional music.'

Jan Young, part of a group of six stitchers in Penicuik, was delighted to find herself stitching the story of the *Scotsman* newspaper, having worked for the organisation for years, eventually as head of the *Evening News* special features department. She got stuck into research, exploring the paper's origins in 1817, when it was a radical independent rag no respectable Edinburgh gent would be seen with. The images she suggested for the panel include a newspaper billboard, a homing pigeon (at one time the paper had its own pigeon loft and used the birds to bring results back from local football matches) and a quotation from David Hume in Teeline shorthand.

Meanwhile, Yvonne Beale, a scientist with a PhD in Genetics, was delighted to be stitching the panel on the cloning of Dolly the Sheep. Yvonne was an undergraduate at St Andrews University when Dolly was cloned, studied for a PhD in the Pathology department at Edinburgh University and worked for the Newcastle Science Festival before taking up her current vocation as a full-time mum. She moved to Orkney with her family while working on the panel.

A keen stitcher, after being taught to sew as a child by her piano teacher, Yvonne was looking for something a bit more challenging than the average embroidery kit. 'When I went

THE SCOTSMAN FOUNDED 1817

to see the Prestonpans Tapestry, I was inspired, and I knew I wanted to work on this. I asked if there was any way I could do this panel and was thrilled when it came in the post. The first thing that struck me when I opened the package was the smell of the wool. It was funny to think that I was going to be turning wool back into a sheep!

'When Dolly's cloning was announced, I went and heard Ian Wilmut (the lead scientist on the project) speaking about it. Back then people were quite concerned about where cloning could go; it was interesting to hear all sides of that debate, and good for me to revisit and research some of these things. Trying to show a science subject in an artistic way is hard, but I have an interest in science-art fusion.'

She was delighted when Andrew asked her for other scientific motifs which could be added to the panel and came up with a diverse range from equations relating to the Higgs boson particle ('How do you put quantum physics in embroidery?'), DNA strands, and a wind turbine to signify advances in renewable energy. 'Scotland has got such a strong scientific heritage of really big discoveries, and it's nice to get the chance to commemorate that in embroidery.'

Jacquie McNally is a costume designer who has worked in theatre, film and television. At the BBC, she worked on the costumes for the *Pride and Prejudice* mini-series, starring Colin Firth and Jennifer Ehle, and has made costumes for Nicole Kidman and Cate Blanchett. But, as an aficionado of all things relating to the 1950s, she was perfectly suited to her panel, 'Pop Music Booms'.

The central image in the design is a classic 1950s couple, dancing on the turntable of a record player, and Jacquie decided she could up the ante. 'I decided to depict the couple as my parents when they met, so I used photographs to copy my mum's hairstyle, and she is wearing a 1950s dress which I have, and my dad has his quiff.' Around them are pop stars of

Opposite.
The Penicuik Team with their panel outside the offices of *The Scotsman.*

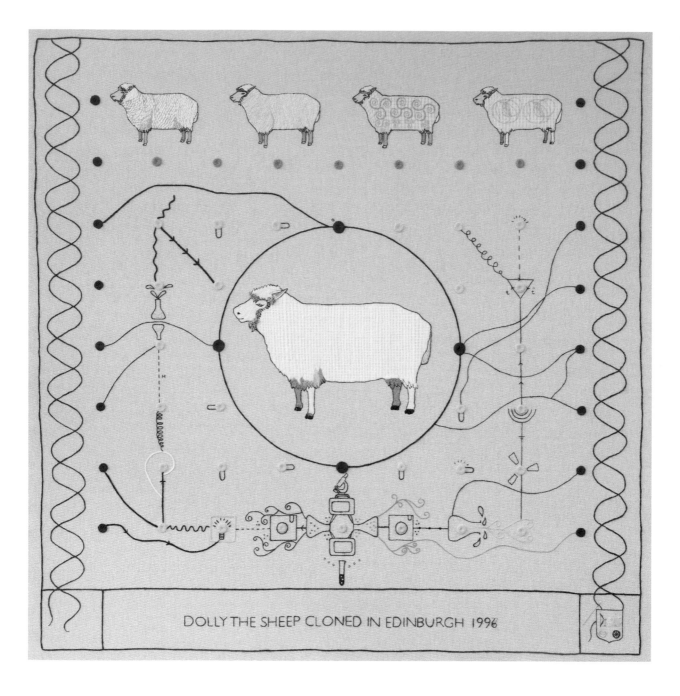

DOLLY THE SHEEP CLONED IN EDINBURGH 1996

POP MUSIC BOOMS

the day: Lulu, Alex Harvey, Elvis Presley – 'because he came to Prestwick. And I love skiffle, so I had to get Lonnie Donegan in there.' The panel became a family affair, because she enlisted her ten-year-old son Charlie to help. 'He only does seed stitch, but he's very good at it. It's probably a bit of a selfish thing, but I think it's lovely to have a bit of your family in something so historical.'

Susie Finlayson also found a way to weave her family into a scene she was stitching about shinty. 'The three figures are all wearing kilts, though I'm not sure if anybody ever played shinty wearing a kilt! The central figure has a green jacket and a red and green kilt which is what my dad wears. Another has a darker top and darker kilt which is like my husband, so I made them into my husband, father and uncle.'

She later volunteered to help with a panel about Fair Isle – as a keen knitter, she couldn't resist the opportunity to stitch Fair Isle jumpers – but she also left a tiny, poignant addition to the design, a helicopter. Her husband, Bruce, who is a subsea engineer, was one of 19 people rescued when a helicopter en route to a drilling rig ditched in the sea west of Fair Isle in October 2012. 'It was all very professionally handled – the pilots got all the guys out, nobody was injured and they all came home the next day – but it was a fairly traumatic experience for us. Perhaps it's so small that unless you know what it is and why it's there you wouldn't notice it, but that's our thing, and it was a big thing to happen.'

Every panel has a story: the miner's wife who embroidered her late husband's tag and his sandwich box; the figure of David Livingstone in the 'Scots in Africa' panel, which was embroidered by one of his descendants; the stitcher whose dog modelled for Queen Victoria's King Charles spaniel; the flea-bite on the neck of a shipyard worker, an affectionate tribute to a stitcher's uncle who brought back fleas from the yards. And who knows how many more. These tiny tributes,

Opposite.
Andrew Crummy's design for Panel 126.

Above, opposite and
pp. 74–75: Many groups
devised their own distinctive
signatures and worked them
into their finished panels.

mementos and private jokes are hidden in the detail, as stitchers do what craftsmen have always done, weaving traces of their own lives into their work.

Life isn't on hold while you're stitching. The Newport on Tay group marked an arrival and a departure in the nine months it took them to complete their tapestry: the joy of a first grandchild, and the loss of a much-loved father-in-law. The Crewel Chicks celebrated their final stitches in hospital as Betty had to go in for minor surgery. And there were several panels returned to the Hub because, for a variety of reasons, their stitchers could not complete them. They were then finished by others.

Then there are the stories which can't be told, stories that cause the ladies at the Hub to exchange knowing glances and chuckle. Stitching is passionate, detailed work in which much time and pride is invested, and not every grouping of people will work smoothly together. Occasional mishaps in the stitching process are recounted on the strict understanding that they won't be repeated. So the secret of David Hume's nose and James Hamilton's leg will have to remain secrets. As Andrew Crummy says: 'The ladies are a force of nature; you don't cross them.'

By Christmas 2012, almost all the kits had been dispatched

to groups, but the list of panels was still growing. Alistair Moffat and Andrew Crummy took the view that, if a strong case could be made for a panel to be added, it should be heard. So when a group of women from Paisley came to them with an idea for a panel, given that town's rich connections with the textile industry, they could hardly refuse.

They had started out as a reminiscence project gathering stories of Paisley between the wars and publishing them on a website. But when the organisers saw the Prestonpans Tapestry, which was exhibited in Paisley Thread Mill Museum, they had a further idea: could they turn their materials into a panel for the Great Tapestry of Scotland? It was felt that, as well as celebrating Paisley during a key period, the panel – which features various aspects of tenement life – also had a wider relevance to the social history of Scotland.

The last panel to be added was a panel on the whaling industry, at the suggestion of Sir Gerald and Lady Margaret Elliot, who provided significant funding for the project from the Binks Trust. Sir Gerald, a former Christian Salvesen chairman, felt that whaling, an important part of the Salvesen enterprise until the 1960s, was a story which deserved to be told. He said: 'Whaling was a major part of the lives of many Scots, particularly in the hungry years after the Second World War.

SOUTHERN HARVESTER

SOUTHERN VENTURER

LEITH HARBOUR, SOUTH GEORGIA

GREAT TAPESTRY OF SCOTLAND Panel No.......... Title..

There is still a lively association of old whalers in Leith and Salvesens employed men from other east coast fishing towns and from the Shetlands. The design for the panel incorporates the names of the two great floating factories on which many men served.'

But the whaling panel arrived at the Hub at a difficult time for Dorie. 'I was very low because I was thinking, "we have no more stitchers; I have no way to contact any more stitchers". It was a beautiful panel, and we all had ideas about how we would stitch it, but our hands were full. And then, out of the blue, I got an email from a girl on Orkney, Rosalind Neville-Smith, saying: "I've just got distinction on an embroidery course, and I would really quite like to take part." I thought it was too good to be true, so I phoned her. I told her that we were thinking how good it would be to use some of the designs from fishermen's gansey jumpers in the panel, and she said, "It's funny you say that; I designed one for my dad and knitted it for him." It was like a little miracle.'

The first panel to arrive back at the Hub in early spring showed an encampment at Cramond circa 8000 BC, and was stitched by a group of weavers in Halflinbarns in East Lothian. The sight of it brought cheer to Dorie, Gillian and the volunteers: in the quality of the stitching and the detail in the landscape, the weavers had produced a fine piece of crewel work. 'Until then, we'd been sending out kits not really knowing what would come back, and getting stressed about the deadline,' says Gillian. 'That was the point when it felt real, when it felt like it was going to happen.'

By June, finished panels were arriving every day. Dorie had given instructions not to iron or treat the linen, and so they arrived just as they had been stitched: creased, some with a dog or cat hair, a few with a faint smell of chips. Volunteers would gather around Dorie's work table to see each new arrival as it emerged from its bag.

Opposite.
The final design for Panel 124.

Panel 6, the first to be finished and returned to The Hub.

I was at the Hub when Muriel Clelland of Trinity Stitchers came to deliver their completed panel, about the Irish immigration to Scotland in the wake of the Great Famine, and to marvel at the work the three women had done mixing colours and textures to make the clothes of the starving Irish look threadbare. The figure in the centre wades across the Irish Sea to Scotland, carrying a woman on his back, and Muriel had the idea of darkening his trousers where they touch the water. It is an ingenious, human touch and one

Above and pp. 80–81: The complex post-stitching process underway at The Hub.

which earned the stitchers the moniker 'the wet trousers group' at the Hub.

Muriel says she and her two fellow stitchers were 'a wee bit sad' to be giving their panel up after 11 months of work. 'At first I wasn't too sure about the subject matter; I'd thought I might get to do some tartan. When we got the panel empty, it seemed not so interesting, but soon we got caught up in it. It tells an important story and we've really grown to love it.'

They were not the only ones to feel a pang of loss when they handed over their completed panel. Ann Gambles and her Dunblane team say they will miss Archie Gemmill. The Smailholm group have said a fond goodbye to their Border Reivers. The tapestries have been part of people's lives for almost a year, the subject of much time and attention. The average number of hours of stitching per full-size panel is 400, but some have spent much more. Kate Edmunds describes spending 37 hours on two square inches of rocks on the James Hutton panel. Another stitcher, working on 'Scotland at the Movies', was heard to remark he'd spent seven hours doing Sean Connery's hair.

After an initial examination, returned panels are taken to the 'wet room' across the hall where they are tacked on to wooden frames edged with carpet gripper to stretch the fabric evenly in all directions and realign the fibres of both linen and wool. Once on the frame, they are sprayed back and front with water using a garden sprayer and remain there for three days, until the fabric is dry. The wet room has a good supply of sticking plasters (for attending to carpet tack injuries), and vodka (which has proven to be the best substance for removing any marks or stains). When I visit, Ramsay Macdonald is leaning nonchalantly against a wall, while David Hume and Jean-Jacques Rousseau are lying flat on the floor next to Queen Victoria. Back next door, sewing machines whirr as the newly stretched panels are backed with cotton, finished and hemmed, ready for hanging either with Velcro strips or wooden batons.

Stitcher Christine Palmer from Blairgowrie had her panel on 'Victoria and Albert at Balmoral' finished and wrapped up ready to return to the Hub when she got a phone call from Andrew Crummy. The amount of white space in the background above the figures of the Queen and Prince had been troubling him, and he'd just had an idea: could she add a pair of swans? The panel was duly unpacked and the swans added. Not only do they complete the composition perfectly, but the symbolism fits: swans mate for life and will mourn a lost partner, as Victoria did Albert.

The Great Tapestry of Scotland has impacted many lives. Many of those who took part describe how their confidence has grown, how it has challenged them and taken them in new directions. Susie Finlayson says she has 'got the bug' and has several ideas for other projects. Costume maker Jacquie McNally, who developed a line of hand-embroidered cushions featuring 1950s pin-ups after working on the Prestonpans Tapestry, feels she might have found a successful business venture. Kate Edmunds says she'll never stitch again, but that makes her friends laugh.

Embroidery is normally a solo activity, but many of the

stitchers on this project have discovered the joy of working in a group. Skills have been shared, artistic muscles flexed. In some cases, after many years of pursuing a hobby alone, people have discovered a body of folk with similar interests. Others have come into their own as organisers, administrators and teachers of others.

Many of the stitchers talk about what it means to them to be part of a project that will be preserved for generations. Needlework is often transitory, but the Great Scottish Tapestry is a work which will survive for posterity. Veronica Ross sums it up: 'I think we could all see that if we'd had an ancestor who was sewing on the Bayeux Tapestry, that would be so exciting. We are creating something that we hope has a long-term future. We'd like to think it will be around for a thousand years. A big part of most of us is thinking: this is part of the nation's history, aren't we lucky to be part of it?'

But the conservation of the tapestry will not happen

Above, opposite and pp. 86–87: One of the largest community arts projects ever undertaken in Scotland, the Great Tapestry has involved over a thousand people from all over the country.

84

automatically. Textiles are notoriously vulnerable – to moths, mites, damp, mildew and more. Whenever the tapestry is exhibited, levels of dampness and exposure to light must be carefully controlled, and appropriate conditions must be maintained when it is stored or transported. These and other challenges will be faced by the team in the months ahead.

Meanwhile, Jan Rutherford and Anna Renz – quite apart from helping to stitch a panel themselves – have reached their fund-raising target, having raised £250,000 to bring the tapestry to its first exhibition. And now there is another target: to raise funds to take the tapestry on tour in Scotland and England, and perhaps, in 2015, to North America. After that, there is the hope that it can find a home where it can be held in trust for the nation and permanently displayed.

Jan Rutherford says: 'Our prime concern is to get it out to the people of Scotland; it's their history and their story. We have more than a thousand stitchers all over Scotland; we have

to make sure it is shown as widely as possible.' As the panels are not joined, it is possible that certain parts of it can be taken to smaller, more remote venues. She says she has been struck throughout by the 'huge interest and huge goodwill' the tapestry generates. 'Wherever you take a panel, people are really surprised at the quality of the stitching and the level of effort people have put in; there is excitement, there is delight.'

The tapestry seems to breed goodwill and induce delight. There is always laughter in the Hub as the women go about their work, even as the deadline approaches and they are working day and night to prepare the panels for exhibition.

Alexander McCall Smith sums it up: 'There's so much joy in this project; it's just filling people with happiness, making it, talking about it – it's a great cornucopia of delight.'

Even as they take pleasure from each completed panel, those involved can only speculate what the cumulative effect will be when all 165 panels are exhibited together. The unveiling of the Great Tapestry of Scotland to the public is a moment of transition. The last thread has been knotted, the last panel stretched, the last piece of Velcro stitched on. It feels like a kind of ending. But in fact it is more like another beginning. The beginning of another chapter of the story.

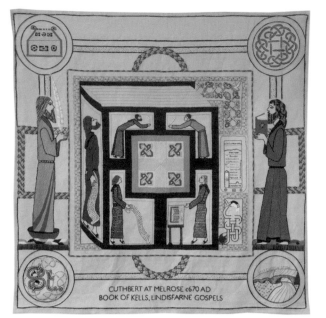

CUTHBERT AT MELROSE c670 AD
BOOK OF KELLS, LINDISFARNE GOSPELS

AND WARP WELL THE LONG THREADS THE BRIGHT THREADS, THE STRONG THREADS, WOOF WELL THE CROSS THREADS

TO MAKE THE COLOURS SHINE

MODERN KILT INVENTED LOCHABER 1723

SCOTLAND IN AFRICA

THE CLYDEBANK BLITZ 1941

Historical Timeline

Almost all of the images and the panels are easy to understand and some have text to help identify who is who and what is what. The Timeline that follows highlights some of the key events and people which feature in The Great Tapestry of Scotland, and is illustrated with a mixture of Andrew Crummy's final designs and finished panels.

Panel 1

4

THE ICE MELTS, SCOTLAND EMERGES, THE FIRST PIONEERS COME

6

ENCAMPMENT AT CRAMOND
SCOTLAND'S FIRST HOUSE AT BARNS NESS, EAST LOTHIAN c8,000 BC

In the beginning was the sea. Scotland was the deposit of a series of ancient collisions. An unimaginably long time ago, around 420 million years BC, the crust of the Earth was moving, forming and reforming enormous continents, filling and draining vast oceans. Part of what became Scotland lay on the rim of a huge landmass and northern England lay on the edge of another. Under the sea between them, the Iapetus Ocean, were the submerged rocks that began to rise, buckle and corrugate as the two continents drew closer. And the angle of the ancient collision is remembered in the north-east to south-west slant of Scotland's geography: the Great Glen, the Highland Boundary Fault, the Midland Valley and the Southern Upland Fault. Most of Scotland's rock formations are of course older and harder than England's.

Very much more recently, the last ice age finally ended sometime around 9000 BC. Glaciers groaned, splintered and ground over the landscape of Scotland like prehistoric sandpaper. Bulldozing boulders, gravel and other deposits, they shaped familiar landmarks like Dumbarton, Stirling and Edinburgh's castle rocks; they scarred out glens and sea lochs, rolling hills and mountains. And when the ice at last drew back and the land greened, people came, the pioneers who first settled Scotland. Every Scot is an immigrant; the only interesting question is when waves of ancestors arrived.

The pioneers left gossamer traces. At Cramond, near Edinburgh, the postholes left by the whippy green rods needed to make a bender tent encampment have been found. And more spectacular, larger postholes were excavated at Barns Ness in East Lothian and interpreted as the earliest substantial house yet found in Scotland.

7

10

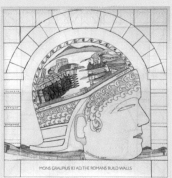

11

In the years around c3000 BC, the greatest revolution in Scotland's history took place. Farmers crossed the North Sea from Europe, and they brought new techniques of cultivating crops and domesticating animals. Life changed utterly and, amongst many spectacular monuments to the productivity of the farmers, were the great stone circles of Orkney and the large timber halls built on the banks of rivers in eastern Scotland at places such as Balbridie, Claish and Kelso.

The Romans followed in AD 79, and in his account of their campaigns, Tacitus described Scotland as a place where it rained a good deal. And where the native warriors were defeated at the Battle of the Graupian Mountain, Mons Graupius, probably below Bennachie in Aberdeenshire.

The Romans also brought Christianity. At Whithorn in Galloway, some time around AD 400, St Ninian founded a church at a place known as Candida Casa, the White House.

12

14

16

Then St Columba came. In the later sixth century, in the wake of Irish warbands who crossed the North Channel to colonise what had been Pictish territory, he founded the monastic community at Iona. Argyll loosely translates as the Coastlands of the Gaels. They brought not only the word of God but also the Gaelic language. Some believe that they are interchangeable and that the latter is indeed the language of Eden.

In the seventh and eighth centuries a Germanic people known as the Angles began to expand out of their coastal enclaves in northern England. Their kings pushed into the Tweed Valley and the Lothians. They brought an early version of English, which developed into Scots, and after finally converting to Christianity, their rulers commissioned great art. Carving, painting and poetry can be seen on the decorated crosses at Bewcastle and Ruthwell. The Angles gave England its name and Scotland its language.

In 793, fell portents were seen. Thunder and lightning rent the air and dragons flew. On the shingle beach of the holy island of Lindisfarne, fearsome warriors rasped their ships up above the high-tide line and raced for the doors of the monastery before the terrified monks could bolt them. The Vikings had sailed into history. Having colonised Orkney, Shetland, the Western Isles, Man and Dublin, they exerted tremendous pressure on the native kingdoms of Britain.

18

19

22

Pressed hard in the west by Viking sea-lords, the kings of Scots and Picts established a power-base in the centre of Scotland at Scone. Under the rule of Constantine II, Scotland began to be seen as a political entity although it was at first called Alba, its Gaelic name.

Anglian domination of the Tweed Valley lasted almost four centuries but it was brought to a brutal end at the Battle of Carham in 1018. With King Owain of Strathclyde as an ally, Malcolm II of Scotland defeated an Anglian army and the frontier began to settle on the Tweed and the watershed ridge of the Cheviot Hills.

David I of Scotland was one of the most successful of medieval kings. Raised at the court of Henry I of England, he brought several orders of reformed monks to the north. In his reign, the four great Border abbeys at Kelso, Melrose, Dryburgh and Jedburgh were founded and their magnificent remains stand testament to both profound belief and a thriving economy

28

DEATH OF ALEXANDER III AT KINGHORN, 1286

30

BANNOCKBURN 1314

32

THE BLACK DEATH, DESERTED FARMS c1350s

At a banquet in Edinburgh Castle on a stormy night in March 1286, King Alexander III was seized by an urgent need to visit his beautiful new wife, Yolande de Dreux. Perhaps the wine had been flowing freely. The only problem was that she was at his manor at Kinghorn in Fife and bad weather had closed in over the Forth. Despite strong advice to the contrary, the king crossed and rode off along the shore path. At Pettycur, he and his horse fell down a steep rocky embankment, and his body was found on the beach the following morning. Having died without an heir, Alexander's uxorious rashness plunged Scotland into the Wars of Independence.

Bannockburn in 1314 was a battle that did turn history. On that famous day, Robert the Bruce's army defied all odds and defeated the much larger force of Edward II of England.

Across Europe plague raged after 1346. It was carried by fleas in the coats of black rats taken westwards in merchant ships. At its peak in 1348–50, the Black Death killed between 75 million and 200 million, about half of the population of Europe. In 1349 a Scottish force planning to raid into England was said to have praised God that the 'foul death of the English' had not affected them. By the end of the year, it is thought that a quarter of the population of Scotland had died. The effect on agriculture was catastrophic and famine followed.

33

40

43

In 1413, the University of St Andrews was formally founded by papal bull, establishing it as the third oldest in the English-speaking world. Courses in divinity, logic, law and philosophy were offered. Lawrence of Lindores was the first in a long line of distinguished Rectors. While England languished with only two universities – at Oxford and Cambridge – until the 18th century, Scotland had four: at St Andrews, Glasgow, Aberdeen and Edinburgh. The historical effects of this imbalance have long been obvious.

The reign of James IV, often seen as Scotland's first renaissance monarch, is also remembered for military disaster. In 1513 the king was killed on Flodden Field as he led the downhill charge of a large Scottish army against an English force under the command of the Earl of Surrey. The slaughter was unprecedented, especially thinning the ranks of the Scottish nobility, but losses were also great on the English side and no invasion of Scotland followed immediately. But Flodden ushered in a century of instability in the south – the age of the Border Reivers.

Reformation came to Scotland in the 1560s and while there was conflict and martyrdoms on both sides, a formal break with the papacy and the Catholic Church was achieved quickly. After the death of Mary of Guise, the Catholic mother of Mary, Queen of Scots, the so-called Reformation Parliament passed acts abolishing the old faith. The First Book of Discipline, partly written by John Knox, set education as a priority. So that the mass of people could read the Bible – the Word of God – for themselves, there would be a school in every parish. This took much sacrifice and many years, but it was eventually achieved.

46

ROBERT CAREY'S RIDE FROM LONDON TO EDINBURGH 1603

47

THE MAKING OF THE KING JAMES BIBLE 1611

50

THE NATIONAL CONVENANT AT GREYFRIARS KIRKYARD 1638

When Elizabeth I of England at last died, Robert Carey rode like the wind from London to Edinburgh to be the first to tell James VI of Scotland that he was to become James I of England and Ireland.

Begun in 1604 and completed seven years later, what is known as the King James Bible was arguably one of the greatest achievements of his reign. Completed by 47 scholars, it set new standards of accuracy and is often hailed as the most influential piece of literature in history.

As the Stewart dynasty became increasingly isolated and the actions of Charles I in refusing to call parliament brought civil war closer and closer, Scotland began to rebel. In particular, the efforts of the king and Archbishop Laud to bring the Churches of Scotland and England together with the introduction of a Book of Common Prayer caused outrage. In 1638, at a ceremony in Greyfriars Kirkyard in Edinburgh, representatives of the nobility, the burgesses and the clergy signed the National Covenant, a document designed to protect the integrity of the Church of Scotland.

56

57

60

As Scotland saw its southern neighbour lay down the foundations of a great empire, the Company of Scotland was formed with the aim of fostering Scottish imperial projects. It raised a staggering sum, £400,000, about a fifth of the wealth of Scotland, in order to colonise part of the Isthmus of Panama, a place known as Darien. An original aim was to dig a canal to link the Atlantic and the Pacific. The scheme was a disaster. Of the 2,500 settlers who sailed from Scotland in 1698, only a few hundred survived and a nation lost a fortune.

The Darien Disaster led indirectly to the Union of the Scottish and English Parliaments. It was claimed that union would help Scotland recover. Despite popular opposition, the Act of Union was passed and a sum of money close to the £400,000 lost in Darien was paid as an ill-disguised bribe known as 'the equivalent'. It was a hostile merger, but by the middle of the 18th century, Scotland's economy was beginning to thrive and many Scots were able to make a career in the sprawling British Empire. After the death of Queen Anne in 1714, the last of the Stewarts had gone – but their ambitions were undimmed.

In the summer of 1745 Bonnie Prince Charlie was rowed up Loch Shiel to join the muster of his Highland army. But only a handful of men greeted him. As hopes faded, the sound of the pipes of Clan Cameron was heard. About a thousand clansmen were led to Glenfinnan by Locheil and the rising had begun. Whatever faults he had, and they appear to have been many, Charles Edward Stuart had charisma and the surprise is not that he failed but that he very nearly succeeded.

62

63

65

The defeat at Culloden in 1746 was the beginning of a long end for the Highland clans, their culture and their language. Gaelic had crossed the North Channel from Ireland with the establishment of the kingdoms of Dalriada and, at its zenith, the language was spoken all over the Highlands and the Western Isles. But as the brutal aftermath of the Jacobite Risings merged into the Clearances, people left the Highlands with Gaelic, a language that they rarely passed on to their children. Now it is spoken by less than 1 per cent of all Scots.

Golf is a Scottish invention. All other claims are entirely insubstantial: at St Andrews and around Edinburgh the modern game began to take shape. The Royal and Ancient Golf Club of St Andrews is probably not the oldest in the world. That honour could probably be claimed by the Royal Burgess Golfing Society of Edinburgh which was founded almost 20 years before, in 1735. But the R&A is the most powerful because it makes the rules. But it does not own a golf course. The Old Course and the others around it are the property of the citizens of the town of St Andrews.

Scottish agriculture had long been hampered by poor technology. The Auld Scots ploo (plough) was built mostly of wood tipped by iron and it took a team of four powerful oxen to pull it through the ground. And because it did not turn the sod completely, it needed an army of plough-followers to break up big clods and pull out weeds. In the 1770s, a Berwickshire blacksmith named James Small perfected the swing-plough. Cast all in iron, it had a screwed shape that turned the sod over completely, could be pulled by one strong horse and guided by one skilled man. It changed cultivation radically, and by doing that it changed the world.

66

72

79

Perhaps the most glittering period in Scotland's history was the second half of the 18th century, known as the Enlightenment. Between 1768 and 1771 *Encyclopaedia Britannica* was established in Edinburgh by William Smellie, a printer, editor and antiquary. It appeared in 100 weekly instalments and could be pithy. The entry for 'Woman' was four words long – 'the female of man'. But it proved popular and a second edition was soon put in train.

In the late 18th and throughout the 19th century, both the Highlands and Lowlands of Scotland slowly emptied of people. Landlords wanted to make profits from sheep or sporting estates, and in the Lowlands, smallholders were cleared as farms grew larger and more cost-effective. The growing cities of the Central Belt offered work for many, but significant numbers reached the quaysides of Glasgow, Greenock and elsewhere and kept going, seeking new lives in North America, Australia, New Zealand and in other developing countries.

The genius of Robert Burns lies in his ability to create poetry that is both complex, heart-breakingly beautiful and accessible to all. At Burns Suppers the world over, the recital, usually from memory, of *Tam o' Shanter* is a highlight. Pure entertainment, it is probably one of the most rollicking, energetic poems ever composed.

82

84

85

Walter Scott's work would be the cause of many journeys to Scotland. First with his long poems, beginning with *The Lay of the Last Minstrel* in 1805, and later with his historical novels, Scott invented the bestseller. His work sold worldwide and he himself became a celebrity feted everywhere he went. His romances swirled around the Scottish hills and glens and were a tremendous stimulus to early tourism.

In 1817 the *Scotsman* newspaper was founded, based in Edinburgh. It quickly grew popular in the east of Scotland as the *Herald*, founded in 1783, dominated in Glasgow and the west.

Whisky production in Scotland was mostly illicit until the early 19th century, made by those anxious to avoid paying excise duty. When George Smith founded the Glenlivet Distillery in 1824, it was unusual for being entirely legal. This made Smith unpopular and he was in the habit of never travelling without a pair of pistols in his belt. He had also to protect his brand from imitators. As it does now, Glenlivet had an excellent reputation.

91

95

96

Queen Victoria and Prince Albert fell in love with Scotland. After their first visit in 1842, they came back often, particularly to the Highlands. Preferring the slightly less rainy climate of Deeside, Albert eventually bought the Balmoral Estate and spent much of his summer shooting deer and other game. Where royalty led the gentry followed and many imitations of Balmoral were built, and tartan and all things Highland became fashionable. Balmorality was born.

The railways not only opened Scotland to tourism inspired by Queen Victoria and Walter Scott, they also became the industrial arteries of the nation. When the Forth Bridge carried the first train from South to North Queensferry in 1890, it was immediately hailed as an engineering marvel. The first structure in Britain to be made from steel, it is also elegant and singular. In any competition to find a man-made icon for Scotland, it would surely win.

By the 19th century the dream of John Knox and the reformers had been realised. There was a school in almost every parish in Scotland and one of the consequences was a high level of mass literacy. At between 70 per cent and 77 per cent, it was highest in Britain in the counties of Caithness and Berwickshire.

102

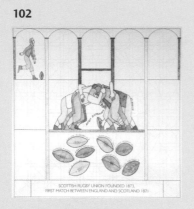

SCOTTISH RUGBY UNION FOUNDED 1873,
FIRST MATCH BETWEEN ENGLAND AND SCOTLAND 1871

111

119

THE BUILDING OF HMS HOOD, BATTLE OF YPRES 1917

The Scottish Rugby Union was at first a Glasgow and Edinburgh affair with all the founding clubs except one coming from the cities. And even though the game's heartland was in the Borders, it continued to be run by clubs of former pupils of Edinburgh and Glasgow schools for many years. The first match between England and Scotland was played in 1871 at Raeburn Place, Edinburgh and the Scots triumphed by a try to nil. It has been downhill ever since.

Born in a one-room cottage near Holytown in Lanarkshire, Keir Hardie had a meteoric rise. From being a miner, he became a union organiser and was then elected as MP for West Ham South in London in 1892. A year later he and others formed the Independent Labour Party. After making a speech in parliament attacking the monarchy, Hardie lost his London seat but was later elected MP for Merthyr Tydfil and Aberdare, a constituency he served for the rest of his life. In the 1906 Liberal landslide, Labour won 29 seats and began to grow into a powerful political force.

Passchendaele, also known as the Third Battle of Ypres, was an offensive launched by the Allies to gain control of the ridges to the south and east of the Belgian city of Ypres. Wet weather bogged down the advance, the German Fourth Army fought back strongly and ultimately British and French troops had to be deployed to Italy to shore up that front after an Austrian victory at Caporetto.

120

122

127

One of the first female doctors to qualify, Elsie Inglis set up medical practice in 1894 and opened a maternity hospital in Edinburgh. She was very unhappy with the standard of medical care for women and that propelled her into the womens' suffrage movement. Elsie Inglis did pioneering work during the First World War but died in 1917 on her return to Britain. The Elsie Inglis Memorial Maternity Hospital was founded in Edinburgh and it continued to innovate in midwifery. Its closure in 1988 was much mourned by many and its warmth and kindness will not be forgotten.

The romantic glory days of amateur sport have no better exemplar than Eric Liddell. The Flying Scotsman won a gold medal for the 400 metres at the Paris Olympic Games of 1924, having refused on religious grounds to run on a Sunday in a heat for the 100 metres, his better event. The year before he had played rugby for Scotland. And at the age of 23, he retired from sport so that he could become a missionary in China. Liddell's extra-ordinary feats were immortalised in the Oscar-winning film *Chariots of Fire*.

Hugh MacDiarmid's masterpiece, *A Drunk Man Looks at the Thistle*, incorporates a passage on the General Strike of 1926, a pessimistic response to its failure. The great lyric is a montage of invective, humour and a collection of themes dealt with in what seem like distinct poems. But it has an authentic voice in Scots, something MacDiarmid imbibed in his youth in the Borders town of Langholm. It begins:

I amna fou sae muckle as tired –
*   deid dune.*
It's gey and hard wark coupin' gless
*   for gless*
Wi' Cruivie and Gilsanquhar and
*   the like,*
And I'm no' juist as bauld as
*   aince I wes.*

128

131

134

The first Labour Prime Minister was a Scot, Ramsay MacDonald. The illegitimate son of a farm labourer, John MacDonald, and a housemaid, Anne Ramsay, he was raised and educated in Lossiemouth. In 1906 he was elected to the House of Commons as a Labour MP for Leicester and in 1911 he became Leader. By the early 1920s Labour had become the main opposition party to the Conservatives and in 1924 King George V called on him to form a minority government with the support of the Liberal Party. He was Prime Minister on three separate occasions. It was an astonishingly meteoric life course for the time.

The first action of the Second World War was fought in the skies above the Firth of Forth as German aircraft attacked the naval base at Rosyth. Scapa Flow in Orkney was also strategically vital for the North Atlantic, and Shetland's proximity to Norway gave rise to the Shetland bus, a series of voyages by fishing boats to help Norwegians flee the Nazi invasion and aid their resistance efforts. On the home front, Prof. John Raeburn organized the 'Dig for Victory' campaign that fed Britain between 1939 and 1945. He encouraged people to convert lawns and flowerbeds into allotments and to keep chickens and pigs in back gardens.

On 6 June 1944, the largest amphibious invasion ever mounted landed on the beaches of Normandy to begin the reconquest of Nazi Europe. Scotland had not only been involved in the preparations and training for the landings, many Scottish soldiers attempted to fight their way up the beaches. Simon Fraser, Lord Lovat, commanded 1 Special Service Brigade and instructed his personal piper, Bill Millin, to play as the troops landed. Under heavy German fire, Millin played 'The Road to the Isles' and 'Hielan' Laddie'. The piper was the only soldier in the Normandy Landings to wear a kilt – it was a Cameron tartan worn by his father in the trenches in the First World War.

135

THE FIRST EDINBURGH FESTIVAL 1947

137

NATIONAL HEALTH SERVICE FOUNDED

138

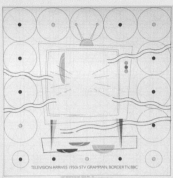

TELEVISION ARRIVES 1950s STV GRAMPIAN BORDER TV BBC

Grim austerity followed the end of the Second World War but one sparkling moment lit the gloom. In 1947 the first Edinburgh Festival took place. The brainchild of Rudolf Bing, the director of Glyndebourne Opera, it brought orchestras, ballet, theatre and exhibitions to the city each August. The official festival programme was immediately joined by the Festival Fringe, eight groups who wanted to add their, largely amateur, performances. The Fringe has come to dominate the Edinburgh Festival and it is now the largest and arguably best arts festival in the world. Edinburgh in August is one of the wonders of the cultural world.

Britain's greatest post-war achievement was the foundation of the National Health Service. This key element of the incoming Labour government's manifesto was difficult to deliver. Many doctors had been used to charging for their services and were unwilling to cooperate, but Aneurin Bevan, the Minister of Health, later said he had 'stuffed their mouths with gold'. In his book *In Place of Fear*, Bevan wrote that 'no society can legitimately call itself civilised if a sick person is denied medical aid because of a lack of means'. That remains the guiding principle of the NHS.

In the 1950s the BBC monopoly was broken with the introduction of ITV in Scotland. STV was first, launching in 1957, and its programmes were what one regulator called 'distressingly popular'. It was based in Glasgow and served the Central Belt and most of the population. Grampian Television set up in Aberdeen in 1961 and, to serve Southern Scotland, Border Television began broadcasting from Carlisle in the same year. These three stations supplied a huge volume of local features, news and drama for about 40 years. Most of this invaluable coverage was swept away in a series of mergers and regulatory changes after 2008.

141

148

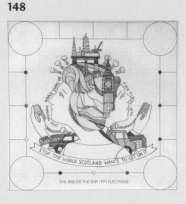

149

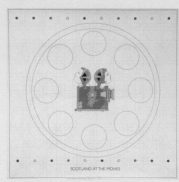

In September 1965 a British Petroleum drilling rig found gas under the bed of the North Sea and four years later oil was also discovered. As the huge Brent and Forties fields came on stream, Britain began to enjoy an unlikely oil boom. Aberdeen became a city of business and high property prices while construction further north at Nigg Bay and terminals at Sullom Voe on Shetland and Flotta on Orkney have supplied employment. Production has begun to decline but vast reserves still remain under the chill waters of the North Sea.

Arguably the most dynamic force for change in post-war Scottish politics has been the Scottish National Party. It has grown from little more than an irrelevant fringe to become the majority party of government in the new Scottish Parliament. Its rise began with Winnie Ewing's stunning victory at the Hamilton by-election of 1967 and continued with the victories of 11 MPs in the 1974 general elections. Ewing has been a central figure in the success of the SNP ever since, winning election after election. Her party forced serious consideration and eventual implementation of Scottish devolution and the resulting Scottish Parliament is now dominated by the SNP.

'The name's Bond, James Bond.' Immortal words, uttered by Sean Connery, which established him as one of the most famous film actors of all time. Other Scots have followed, such as Ewan McGregor, Brian Cox, Kelly Macdonald, Tom Conti and Tilda Swinton. Behind the camera, Alexander Mackendrick, Bill Forsyth and Lynne Ramsay have directed memorable work. And one of the most commercially successful films of all time, *Braveheart*, told the story of a Scottish hero William Wallace.

150

151

155

Dashed hopes and overblown optimism characterise one of the most calamitous episodes in Scotland's sporting history. Throughout the 1960s and 1970s, Scotland's football team had occasionally been inspired and when they left for the 1978 World Cup in Argentina, crowds filled Hampden Park and lined the route to Prestwick Airport. They believed they could win the trophy. An opening defeat by Peru made that seem unlikely and a dismal draw against Iran meant that they had to defeat a brilliant Dutch team by three clear goals to avoid going out of the competition. Finally playing the football of which they were capable, they beat Holland 3–2, Archie Gemmill scoring one of the greatest goals of all time. From the ridiculous to the sublime.

The Miners' Strike of 1984/85 seemed like the end of an era. In the 1970s the National Union of Mineworkers had humbled a Conservative government but Margaret Thatcher was determined that history would not repeat itself. After stockpiling fuel and deploying police forces all over the country, she succeeded in forcing the miners back to work and pushing through a programme of closure. Many famous collieries in Scotland shut down in the year following – Monktonhall, Bilston Glen, Polmaise, Seafield and Longannet. There are no working deep mines left in Scotland and heavy industry has also been drastically reduced.

When Sheena Wellington sang Robert Burns' great lyric, 'A Man's A Man For A' That', at the opening of the Scottish Parliament in 1999, her beautiful, crystal voice caught the mood of the nation perfectly. All rejoiced on 1 July, Scotland's day. And setting party allegiances aside, all agreed that Winifred Ewing MSP should preside over the opening session and her memorable words were: 'The Scottish Parliament, adjourned on the twenty-fifth day of March in the year 1707, is hereby reconvened.'

160

THE GREAT TAPESTRY OF SCOTLAND

History is about change, and change always involves loss. Memories faded into half-forgotten myths or evaporated entirely as history rumbled across the landscape. But moments such as the opening of the Scottish Parliament may be seen as a pause, and the freeze-frame of a tapestry panel an attempt to catch that moment and hold it still. The Great Tapestry of Scotland may never end, may be added to over the coming times, but this version pauses with a Parliament of the Ancestors, the men and women who helped make Scotland, and a Parliament for the Future. Two panels show leaders: the four Presiding Officers and the four First Ministers who have held office since 1999. Other living Scots are there, and our ancestors below and beside them. They are all flanked by the stitchers, the women and men who not only made the tapestry but also made a version of Scotland when they first picked up their needles and thread. It is their story and our story.

List of Panels